SPEED!

MILITARY VEHICLES

Jenifer Corr Morse

BLACKBIRCH PRESS, INC.
WOODBRIDGE, CONNECTICUT

To William G. Corr
–JCM

Published by Blackbirch Press, Inc.
260 Amity Road
Woodbridge, CT 06525
Web site: www.blackbirch.com
e-mail: staff@blackbirch.com

© 2001 Blackbirch Press, Inc.
First Edition

Printed in Belgium

10 9 8 7 6 5 4 3 2 1

Photo Credits
Cover (top left and bottom right), pages 1, 4-5, 14-15: Corel Corporation; cover (top right), pages 10-13: United Defense photos; cover (bottom left), page 18: Advanced Vehicle Systems; pages 7, 9: courtesy of General Dynamics Land Systems; pages 16-17: courtesy of Lockheed Martin; page 21: courtesy U.S. Army; page 22: courtesy The Boeing Company.

Library of Congress Cataloging-in-Publication Data
Morse, Jenifer Corr.
   Military Vehicles / by Jenifer Morse.
      p. cm. — (Speed!)
Includes index.
   ISBN 1-56711-471-7
   1. Armored vehicles, Military—United States—Juvenile literature. 2. Vehicles, Military—United States—Juvenile literature. [1. Armored vehicles, Military. 2. Vehicles, Military.] I. Title II. Speed!
(Woodbridge, Conn.)

UG446.5 .M595 2001
623.7'47—dc21
                                                00-011918

Contents

This 63-ton battle tank can cruise along at 42 miles (67 km) per hour.

M1A1 Abrams Main Battle Tank

A powerful tank that cruises

The M1A1 Abrams main battle tank is a powerful fighting machine. Even though this giant tank weighs 63 tons, it is capable of cruising at a top speed of 42 miles (67 km) per hour. With its gas turbine engine that produces 1,500 horsepower, the M1A1 is able to accelerate from 0 to 20 (0 to 32 km) miles per hour in just 7 seconds. It is also able to drive for 275 miles (442 km) before refueling!

A four-person crew—including a commander, gunner, loader, and driver—rides inside the M1A1. It has a ground clearance of 19 inches (48 cm), and is able to cross obstacles up to 3.5 feet (1 m) high. It is also able to cross trenches up to 9 feet (3 m) deep.

The U.S. Army first used M1 series battle tanks in 1980. The M1A1—an updated version of the original M1—was first produced in 1985. Since their development, approximately 8,800 M1s and M1A1s have been produced for the armies of the United States, Egypt, Kuwait, and Saudi Arabia.

Fast Fact

★ Length:	32.3 ft	(9.8 m)
★ Height:	8 ft	(2.4 m)
★ Width:	12 ft	(3.6 m)

The M1A1 is equipped with several weapons. The main gun on board is a 120mm M256 Smooth Bore Cannon. The commander fires a .50 Cal M2 machine gun, while the loader uses a 7.62 M240 machine gun.

Wolverine with Heavy Assault Bridge

Can install and remove a giant bridge in just 15 minutes

The Wolverine is a modified M1 Abrams battle tank that is capable of installing a temporary bridge for troops that need to cross difficult terrain. The Heavy Assault Bridge is carried on top of the Wolverine. When needed, the Wolverine can install an 85-foot- (26-m) long bridge in just 5 minutes! This 12-ton bridge is made of 4 sections and measures 13 feet (4 m) wide. Once installed, a 70-ton vehicle can cross the bridge 5,000 times at 10 miles (16 km) per hour!

A two-person crew rides in the Wolverine. All of the controls for operating the bridge are located inside the vehicle, so the crew members are always protected when they are moving the bridge. After the bridge has been crossed, the crew can retrieve it in less than 10 minutes. The same bridge can be launched and retrieved up to 2,200 times before it needs repair.

Even though the Wolverine system is a modified tank, it still has many impressive features of a standard battle tank. It has a 19-inch (48-cm) ground clearance, and can cross 3-foot- (1-m) high obstacles and 8.5-foot- (2.7-m) deep trenches with its sturdy treads.

> ## Fast Fact
>
> **With an engine capable of producing 1,500 horsepower, the 68-ton Wolverine can reach a top speed of 45 miles (72 km) per hour.**

The Wolverine is able to install an 85-foot-
(26-m) long bridge in only 5 minutes.

Advanced Amphibious Assault Vehicle (AAAV)

Speeds over land and sea

The Marine Corp's Advanced Amphibious Assault Vehicle (AAAV) is truly a versatile machine. It can transport troops over both land and sea at top speeds. While on the move, this armored vehicle is also able to provide fire support to troops.

The AAAV can carry 17 combat troops, and their equipment, to land from a ship stationed up to 25 miles (40 km) from shore. In waves up to 3 feet (1 m) high, the AAAV can reach a top speed of 25 miles (40 km) per hour. For this bulky vehicle to reach such a high speed, it must become more aerodynamic. When operating in water, the AAAV retracts its treads and suspension system and covers the area with smooth plates. This allows the water to flow around the vehicle without slowing it down.

As the AAAV approaches shore, it reduces speed and retracts its cover plates. Then, in about 10 feet (3 m) of water, it lowers its treads and suspension system. It comes to shore at about 10 miles (16 km) per hour. On land, the AAAV can run at a top speed of 45 miles (72 km) an hour.

> ## Fast Fact
>
> The ability to move over both land and sea has a steep price. It costs about $6.5 million to produce an Advanced Amphibious Assault Vehicle.

The AAAV can speed across land and through water.

M88A2 HERCULES

Can tow a 70-ton vehicle at 26 miles (41.8 km) per hour

The M88A2 HERCULES is a heavy recovery vehicle that is used to tow broken-down battle tanks and other combat vehicles out of danger. It also rescues troops and is equipped to fix vehicles that are not severely damaged. This 70-ton machine can tow a 70-ton M1A1 Abrams main battle tank at 26 miles (41.8 km) per hour!

The HERCULES is a 70-ton towing machine that can cruise at 26 miles (41.8 km) per hour while pulling another tank.

The M88A2 HERCULES uprights an overturned M1 Abrams tank.

The HERCULES has a three-person crew and a ground clearance of 16 inches (40 cm). It can carry 430 gallons (1,514 l) of fuel and cruise for up to 300 miles (483 km) before refueling. This machine can be transported throughout the world by air, highway, and railway.

HERCULES stands for Heavy Equipment Recovery Combat

Fast Fact

★ Length: 28.2 ft   (8.6 m)
★ Height: 10.5 ft   (3.2 m)
★ Width: 12 ft   (3.7 m)

When it is not towing another vehicle, the HERCULES can reach a maximum of 30 miles (48 km) an hour. It gets its strength from a JP-8 tuned engine that produces 1,050 horsepower.

Utility Lift and Evacuation System. It is a fairly new design, and was created to replace the M88A1 Medium Recovery Vehicle. The older vehicles could not pull the new, heavier M1A1 Abrams tanks that are now used in battle. The new HERCULES can lift 40% heavier loads, and drive 25% faster than the old M88A1. More armor was added to the HERCULES to increase the safety of the crew. As the vehicle became heavier, it had an easier time safely pulling and controlling large loads.

Crusader

Automated vehicle that saves time and personnel

The Crusader system—formerly known as the Advanced Field Artillery System—contains some of the Army's most hi-tech instruments. The system is actually made up of two vehicles—a self-propelled howitzer (SPH) and a re-supply vehicle (RSV). Its main purpose is to provide artillery support to troops on the battlefield. Both vehicles have robotic handling systems that decrease the time and crew needed to resupply.

Capable of driving up to 42 miles (67 km) an hour, the self-propelled howitzer is operated by 3 crew members. Even though it looks like a tank, the SPH plays a very different role in battle. Instead of sitting on the front lines, the SPH is usually located about a mile back. That's because the crew does not have to find its target to fire. The crew gets the location of its target digitally transmitted to its onboard computer by radar or by other soldiers. Based on

> ## Fast Fact
>
> The Crusader has an incredibly accurate firing system. It is able to hit a target from up to 18 miles (30 km) away.

the message it receives, the computer then recommends a weapon to fire and sets up for discharge. If the crew approves the plan, the computer fires the weapon within 15 to 20 seconds.

A resupply port is located in the back of the SPH and connects to the RSV. A completely automated system brings weapons from the RSV to the SPH and loads them in the proper storage spaces. This convenient system allows crew members to remain safely in the SPH while they get a new supply of weapons from the other vehicle.

The Crusader's onboard computer can locate enemy targets and recommend weapons to fire.

HMMWVs can drive over almost any surface and in all kinds of weather.

HMMWV

A multi-purpose, high performance military vehicle

The HMMWV, or High Mobility Multipurpose Wheeled Vehicle, is used by the U.S. Army and Marines for a variety of tasks. Different models of these lightweight trucks serve as command vehicles, field ambulances, bases for special weapons, and carriers for both troops and ammunition. The military relies on the HMMWV because of its power and performance. Its V8, 6.2-liter diesel engine produces 150 horsepower, allowing the truck to reach a top speed of 55 miles (88.5 km) per hour. The HMMWV is also equipped with a three-speed automatic transmission and four-wheel drive.

Fast Fact

- ★ Length: 15 ft (4.5 m)
- ★ Height: 6 ft (1.8 m)
- ★ Width: 7 ft (2.1 m)

The average weight of this truck is about 5,200 pounds (2,358 kg). Depending on the type of vehicle, HMMWVs can pull from 1,900 to 5,300 pounds (862 to 2,404 kg).

The HMMWV is very useful because it is easy to transport by plane, and can be dropped just about anywhere. It has wheels that can drive over almost any surface and in any type of weather.

The truck can hold 25 gallons (95 l) of gas and can drive for about 300 miles (563 km) before refueling. Each HMMWV costs around $50,000. They were originally acquired by the military to replace the old M151 jeeps.

MEWSS

High-speed vehicle with super communication and reception power

The U.S. Marine Corp uses the MEWSS to improve their own communications and alter enemy signals. The MEWSS—which stands for Mobile Electronic Warfare Support System—consists of a communication system that is mounted on top of a Light Armored Vehicle (LAV). The LAV can reach a top speed of 62 miles (100 m) per hour on land and 6 miles (9.6 km) per hour in water. That's pretty impressive for a 27,000-pound (12,247-kg) vehicle!

The main communication system of the MEWSS is called the Intelligence and Electronic Warfare Common Sensor (IEWCS). It has several antennae, as well as a 37-foot (11.3-m) telescopic mast that can rotate a full 360 degrees. The MEWSS uses this system to communicate with other troops, jam and intercept enemy communication, collect data, and locate enemy forces.

The weapons aboard the MEWSS include a M257 smoke grenade launcher and a M240E machine gun. It carries 16 grenades and 1,000 rounds of ammunition.

◉ Fast Fact ◉

- ★ Length: 21.6 ft (6.6 m)
- ★ Height: 8.7 ft (2.6 m)
- ★ Width: 8.2 ft (2.5 m)

The MEWSS generally carries a four-person crew, including a driver, a commander, and two electronic operators.

The MEWSS sits on top of an LAV,
which can reach a top speed of 62
miles (100 km) per hour on land.

IFAV

The fanciest car in the military

The IFAV is really a Mercedes Benz that can reach a top speed of 96 miles (154 km) per hour.

The Interim Fast Attack Vehicle, or IFAV, is manufactured by Daimler-Chrysler and is actually a Mercedes Benz! This speedy military vehicle can reach a top speed of 96 miles (154 km) an hour on both paved roads and country terrain.

The IFAV can carry a driver, a commander, and up to four passengers. The body of the vehicle is made with shrapnel-proof armor that was tested with grenades. The driver's side is equipped with night vision.

The IFAV has been tested with several weapons mounts, including a M19 40mm grenade launcher and a 50-caliber machine gun.

Sixty-two newly acquired IFAVs were delivered to the Marine Corp in December of 1999 to replace their old M151 jeeps. In addition to being faster, the IFAV is more compatible with most other Marine machinery because it uses diesel fuel. Once in service, these vehicles will fill several roles for the U.S. military. Marines plan to use the IFAV for fast attacks, ambulance service, communication, and command duties. Each IFAV costs $65,000.

Fast Fact

- ★ Length: 15 ft   (4.6 m)
- ★ Width: 5.3 ft   (1.6 m)
- ★ Weight: 7,760 lbs   (3,520 kg)

The IFAV can climb up an 80% grade and can change from two-wheel to four-wheel drive while in motion. The IFAV can also drive for up to 300 miles (483 km) before refueling.

DEUCE

One of the Army's most powerful earthmovers

The DEUCE—Deployable Universal Combat Earthmover—is quickly becoming a great asset to the U.S. Army. It is used for several bulldozing duties, including clearing, leveling, and excavating. It helps troops build airstrips, roads, and places to set up position.

In addition to its many standard bulldozing features, the DEUCE is speedy and can drive at the same pace as other military equipment. This means that, unlike other bulldozers, no other vehicles are necessary to tow it along.

When DEUCE is done bulldozing, the operator simply flips a switch to move the machine into driving mode. The DEUCE's power-shift transmission means that one setting is used for powerful earthmoving, and then a six-speed automatic transmission is used for driving. In driving mode, DEUCE can drive 35 miles (56.3 km) an hour.

> ## ⊃≣Fast ≣Fact ⊂
>
> **Once the machine is turned on, DEUCE is ready to dig in less than a minute. This means that the crew's time is not wasted while the machine warms up.**

Another of DEUCE's unique features is its rubber track. Most other construction equipment has steel tires that damage asphalt roads. DEUCE's rubber track allows it to travel on several different surfaces. This machine is also easier to control because it has a steering wheel, brakes, and an accelerator that is similar to one found in a car.

The DEUCE is a powerful, heavy-duty construction vehicle.

The Avenger is fast, accurate, and highly mobile, which makes it a very effective weapon.

Avenger

Fast-moving surface-to-air missile system

The Avenger was created because the U.S. Army had a powerful surface-to-air missile and needed to make it mobile. The quick and powerful High Mobility Multipurpose Wheeled Vehicle (HMMWV)—which can cruise at a top speed of 60 miles (97 km) per hour—was chosen to transport the missile system. The Avenger Pedestal Mounted Stinger system was mounted on top of the HMMWV. It is used to shoot down enemy cruise missiles, helicopters, and low-flying aircraft.

The weapons system can rotate a complete 360 degrees. Once the turret is locked into place it will not move, even if the vehicle changes direction. Because the view is so good from the turret, the gunner does not need to rely on a computer to track or engage a weapon.

Fast Fact

★ Length:	16.3 ft	(5 m)
★ Height:	8.8 ft	(2.7 m)
★ Width:	7.2 ft	(2.2 m)
★ Weight:	8,300 lbs	(3,765 kg)

At night, or during bad weather, the crew of the Avenger can use forward-looking infrared radar, a laser range finder, and video tracking to find their target.

A special radio is also onboard the Avenger. If it is tuned to the Army air defense command system, the system can be programmed to respond to images that appear on the radar screen. If the gunner accepts the target, the laser system will automatically fix on it. The gunner then tracks the target and fires. This process is called "slew to cue."

Glossary

aerodynamic: designed to move through the air very easily and quickly

grade: the amount of slope on a road

horsepower: a unit for measuring the power of an engine

terrain: ground, or land

turret: a structure on a tank that holds one or more guns; it usually rotates so that the gun can be fired in different directions

For More Information

Books

Abramovitz, Melissa. *Main Battle Tanks* (Land and Sea). Mankato, MN: Capstone Press, 2001.

Black, Michael A. *Tank: The M1A1 Abrams* (High-Tech Military Weapons). Danbury, CT: Children's Press, 2000.

Green, Michael. *Military Trucks.* Mankato, MN: Capstone Press, 1997.

Web Site

United Defense

Learn more about the different vehicles the United States military uses—
http://www.uniteddefense.com/markets/index.htm

Index